Advance Praise for *The F*

"*The Family Plot,* by Linda McCauley Freeman, pulses with life. Poems rich in sense detail portray one American girlhood, one American family, in all of its joy and its sorrow. McCauley Freeman understands that joy and sorrow often coexist inside one moment, and that this moment lives on, like 'one of those [souvenir] photos/vendors take without asking, then charge you to keep.' One poem recalls a father bursting into his boisterous sons' locked room: 'the hinges popped/and our father became for a moment//Aladdin, riding the door to the floor/in a flash of dust.' Likewise, *The Family Plot* arrives on the poetry scene, and not a minute too soon."
—Suzanne Cleary, author of *Crude Angel* (BkMk Press, 2018)

"In *The Family Plot,* Linda McCauley Freeman describes the difficult and at times dangerous interiors and landscapes of childhood secrets—of a beloved grandmother who is not who she is believed to be, of a mother's 'jade-crowned heart, / green, like her eyes,' of a sister who is 'first to get everything,' of little brothers who 'shake coffee cans of buttons,' and 'hurled / steak knives at my unflinching body,' of a father buried 'up to his neck,' and of a grandfather's 'big hand, blue-veined/rough.' Honest and brave, these poems chronicle a family's wounds and a child's survival."
—Beth Copeland, author of *Blue Honey* (Broadkill River Press, 2017), winner of the 2017 Dogfish Head Poetry Prize

"McCauley Freeman's, *The Family Plot,* is brave and unsettling. In these poems the poet unlocks words from her 'diary with the tiny key' to reveal family dysfunction, ancestral secrets, insecurities and, ultimately, the love she finds real and satisfying. Through the poems in this collection, we stand with the poet as she looks deep into the cracked mirror of her early years and finds there the material for reconciliation and redemption.

"Sharp images and steely language make the reader feel the barbs and splinters of growing up in a large family, where despite the noise of a full house, the poet felt alone and forgotten, 'I picked up my mother's coffee cup / from the kitchen table, put my mouth / over the cold red imprint of lips.' The collection abounds with characters that are quirky and flawed, 'The year we are no longer friends / she will get a nose job.' 'Aunt Cary and Aunt Venera visited as a pair / my entire life.' In 'The Photo,' McCauley Freeman describes the framed photo of her parents kept on her father's dresser, 'And the jagged cut between them, / where he's scissored me out of the picture.' In this collection we witness the reassertion of the forgotten child into her own gutsy narrative, stronger, wiser, and linguistically triumphant."

—Julia Morris Paul, author of *Shook* (Grayson Books, 2015) and *Staring Down the Tracks* (Poetry Box, 2020)

The Family Plot

The Family Plot

Poems

Linda McCauley Freeman

BWP

Backroom Window Press
Saint Louis, Missouri

These poems, or earlier versions, appeared in the following journals:

"A Letter to My High School Sweetheart," *Love Letters* (Sweetycat Press)
"Body, Shame, Beauty, Theft," *I Sing the Body Anthology* (Juventud Press)
"I Am," *Mom Egg Review* (reprints *Trailer Park Quarterly* and *Waves*)
"I Was Older," *Speckled Trout Review*
"Jones Beach, 1968," *Califragile*
"Mother," *Adanna Literary Journal*
"On Taking Our 84-Year-Old Dad to Six Flags," *Life is a Roller Coaster* (Kind of a Hurricane Press)
"Plastic Pearls," *Pif Magazine*
"Silent/Death" (published as "The Grandfather"), *Word Gumbo*
"Still Life," *Tomorrow and Tomorrow*
"The Photo," *Dandelion Review*
"Two-Story House," *50-Word Stories*
"We Were Young Together," *The Poet Anthology Series: Friends & Friendship*
"What I Learned in Catholic School," *Songs of Eretz Poetry Review*

First Edition

Text and titles: Century Schoolbook
Cover design by Linda McCauley Freeman. Photo provided by the author.

1 2 3 4 5 6 7 8 9 10

Printed in the United States of America.
Library of Congress Control Number: 2022931749
ISBN: 978-1-7379872-2-2

Backroom Window Press
2911 S. Compton Avenue
Saint Louis, MO 63118
https://bwpress.org

For my family,
who individually and collectively
made me who I am today.

For my husband,
who loves me that way.

Contents

I

II

III

IV

V

VI

VII

I

Forgotten

I was told to wait, so I am waiting.

All my kindergarten classmates vanish
into parents' big-finned beasts.

Mothers, mid-flight, ask—
Are you sure someone is coming?

I nod to each one. Stand like a toy soldier
outside the school gate.

My eyes search up and down the city street.

The light on the corner keeps turning.
Green then red, green then red.

Cars I don't know come and go.

The last boy leaves,
glances at me, walks away.

I miss him,
miss the someone else,
someone to take my hand, wait with me,
know I am only four going on five,
small even for small.

I don't wear a watch or know
what the big and little hands mean.

I don't know why I am still alone,

still waiting not to be
what I would fear
for the rest of my life.

Pink Rosary with a Silver Cross

I didn't know yet that the twins were boys
or how they'd appear out of the mountain
Mommy had become or why my sister
asked me daily if I'd live upstairs with Grandma
if Mommy died. She seemed fine, though round
and tired on the couch she didn't rise from
for three months. The lady from church cooked
and cleaned, scrubbing the floor on hands and knees
as if in prayer. The day she left, she placed in my palm
rosary beads coiled in a woven wire case—
glistening and cold.

I Was Older

Singing to myself and to the mud pie
for our big sister's seventh birthday,
I didn't notice Paul balancing
on the sandbox edge, though I was
supposed to be watching him.

When he fell, his perfect head smashing
into the sharp concrete wall, I heard only
his cry, not mine as I jumped up
and sheared my skin on the metal shelf.

We walked up the driveway, wailing.

My thigh throbbed with each step
our little legs could barely make.
Paul in front, his overalls, blue and white
stripes that puckered like a seersucker suit.
His left strap fallen off his shoulder,
his right hand holding his head, leaking
blood in bright rivers.

Inside the brick house my mother grabbed
a kitchen towel to hold his head in,
screamed for her mother to come downstairs
and watch my sister and me
while the lady next door drove them
to the hospital, worried his blood
might stain her white upholstery.

When I showed my grandmother
my torn thigh, she grumbled,
I have better things to worry about.

I picked up my mother's coffee cup
from the kitchen table, put my mouth
over the cold red imprint of lips.

Two-Story House

Shaded Bronx sidewalks
children shouting
and the green Buick
that was second base.

Upstairs Grandma left
her teeth on the lace doily
next to the water glass
and empty pill bottles.

What she had threatened,
she had done.

Ambulance took her away.
My father brought her back.

Jones Beach, 1968

I

Adam runs before the waves
touch him. Peter, his twin,
pudgy and blond, sits squarely

on crushed shells, laughs
as water rolls over his belly.
Paul piles sand over our father,

erases all of him from the beach
except his head, which he covers
with a bright blue towel.

As my sister and I walk by, timid
in our red bikinis, my father erupts
from the earth, roaring,

sand- and sun-blistered arms
pull us in. We tackle the great
monster emerging.

II

We have buried our father
up to his neck.

My bikini bottom sags with sand.
I waddle to the ocean, scurry

squealing into the bitter Atlantic,

which seizes me, sucks me,
plunges me headfirst, cheek scraping
shells and sand, saltwater up my nose,

till I rise, gasping, blind,
water tearing from me,

and my father lifts me,
saves me, carries me
away.

Hot Dog Day

They lined up for them:
the dollar-fifty dog in its bun,
milk in the red cardboard pint,
a single bag of chips. I wanted,
not the food, but what it meant,
what others had, could afford
to have, the one day a month
in our small Catholic school
my parents scraped to pay for,
could not afford even this extra
divided among five children,
this one day when everyone
abandoned lunch boxes,
flaunted their identical food,
my lunch box still packed, hidden,
my sister saying, *I'm not hungry,*
my brother saying, *I don't like hot dogs,*
me saying nothing, the twins
too little to know the burning
inside, the hollow unfilled.

Pen Mark on a White Cotton Blouse

It didn't matter to my mother
how it got there, just that it was big
and blue and cut through the white
in a crude circle near the shoulder.
But the image of Sister Joan
throwing the felt-tip pen at me
stained indelibly.

What I Learned in Catholic School

Fold each finger over the other,
like your uniform pleats, and sing out:
Good morning, Sister Mary of the Rosary,
when the principal appeared.

Never touch the host, but peel it
from the roof of your mouth with your tongue
while covering your face, pretending to pray.

Hold it in or pee in your panties
rather than risk raising your hand.

Receive a gold star on your paper: you're smart.
(None means you aren't.)

Make up sins to tell the priest
during confession to have something to say.

Drink spoiled milk when Sister Joan
makes you, even after you told her.

Be a good girl at home
and quiet when Grandpa comes
downstairs and touches you,
down there.

Silent

big hand,
blue-veined
rough
settles where
it should not

at nine even I know this

cold kitchen stove
my back against it
grandfather's
vinegar breath

my bright yellow
Kellogg's cereal bowl
floating
upside down in dishwater

an island
I can't escape to.

Death

mother
struggling
to pull on black rubber boots

she must go tell her mother
that grandfather is dead

brothers and sister watch
father tries to help

I pretend

to be
sad, hug
my 12-year-old body,

blue sparks bursting
like the 4th of July.

Visiting My Good Grandparents

Driving over the George Washington Bridge,
my father always said his father helped build it.
I'd picture my grandfather holding his breath, cheeks billowing
as he lashed big beams to the river floor.

They lived three blocks from Palisades Amusement Park.
Pink cotton candy and my grandmother holding my hand
so tightly I couldn't get lost.

Sometimes I'd stay over, become an only child.

I'd cuddle their two white poodles ringed with jeweled collars—
the only dogs I wasn't afraid of,
inhale my grandfather's pipes,
spin the wooden carousel that held them, watch
the blue hula girl dance as he flexed his arm.

I was small enough to sleep on his green recliner, pillowed
with poodles, my face buried in the fabric of his smell.

In their bedroom off the kitchen behind a curtain
was the biggest bed I'd ever seen. I made a boat of that bed,
sailed with the covers.

I thought potatoes came from a box, corn cold from a can,
until my grandmother mashed potatoes and steamed corn-on-
    the-cob.

I loved her garden smell, her blond, blond hair held by gold
barrettes, her red bow lips, her eyebrows—those drawn

delighted arches.

I didn't know she wasn't my real grandmother.

After my grandfather died, my father stopped taking us
to the New Jersey apartment. For years I thought of
the red double-decker miniature bus on her kitchen shelf.
It reminded me of Trolley in the Neighborhood of Make Believe.

If only it would come get me, so I could see her again.

My Purple Bedroom in Our New House

At my window each morning I watch
factory workers walk from the subway,
speaking so many languages,
and then troop back at night,
the streetlight illuminating each in turn.

Tomorrow is the first day at my new school.
I don't have my uniform yet, so
most of my closet is strewn on the bed,
inside out, crumbled, and deflated rejects.

The winner glistens on the closet door,
its white peter-pan collar shy
against the dress's bold flowers,
colors so loud I could hide inside.

I brush the velour shapes till my fingers prickle,
as if each petal were a promise
of my own blossoming.

Second Oldest's Blues

My little brothers shake
coffee cans of buttons: cha-cha-cha-ing
   in the kitchen. I rattle replies
from the living room.
   Another game I invented
to keep them from killing
   each other or me
until Mom comes home from wherever.

*

Crammed in the station wagon
   to drop my sister off at her shrink,
jealous I couldn't go.

*

My sister, first to get everything:
   her period, breasts, our parents.
I was not even her shadow.
   The dependable Chevy to her Jaguar.
I prayed to be sick to be noticed.

*

On the couch with a book
   and bag of Oreos, the cookie's black crumbs:
frozen ants on my shirt.

Locked

What does the mouth hold in?
My mother standing at the stove, boiling,
her green eyes on the swirling saucepan,
as if she could hurl it at the five of us,
locked into a life she wasn't born to live,
into the time she was born into.

What does the mouth hold in?
Biting my lip, afraid to raise my hand
though I thought I knew the answer.
My sister blaring her radio, screaming at us,
my brothers beating each other up,
my father bewildered by it all.
I had my diary with the tiny key.
My words locked inside.

What does the mouth hold in?
My tongue locked against my teeth.
Still.

II

Body, Shame, Beauty, Theft

School is over for the summer.
It is the worst time of year.

I am fifteen and believe my body
indistinguishable from a pencil.

My best friend, Lisa, shows off
her new yellow bikini and blossomed body.

I lie on her bed

thinking of all the suits I tried
strewn in dressing room stalls,

the $65 padded purple one
I stuffed deep inside my purse.

When we go to the beach I hide under towels.
She has grown so beautiful men stare at her.

I walk slightly behind
so I don't disappoint their view.

She tries to make me feel better by calling
herself ugly. The year we are no longer friends

she will get a nose job.

Hair

My sister hated the thick Italian army
that marched from her head, advanced
across her upper lip. She fought valiantly,

bleached her face so raw she couldn't leave
the house for weeks; leaned low over
the ironing board smoothing the hot iron

over a dishrag over her hair, the acrid
smell, tattered remains of hair
and her howls throughout the house.

She refused to cut it, instead hid it under
a red bandanna. I was the one
with "good" hair. It wasn't enough

that I had stolen her status as only child
years before. Now I went to school
with barely a glance at my hair. It was

too stringy if you asked me. But if you asked
my sister, I had been blessed by the gods
and she had once again been forsaken.

Minority

Trying to fit in
at the rollicking fundamentalist camp

my mother sent me to so I would
know what it felt like to be a minority,

morning prayers erupting into tears,
vows, shouts and screams, my catholic

good-girl-heart pounding; my hands clenched
in prayer to whom I was never sure, I just didn't

want to burn in whosever's hell I was in that summer
for the next year it was Jewish camp where I'd steal

challah from the kitchen and explain my last name
by saying my father isn't Jewish, which wasn't a lie,

and pray that no one would see the crucifix my mother
tucked into my suitcase, but that was next summer,

this summer I must survive hellfire and brimstone
and repent to be saved because here confessions

are unheard nor will they be in my next summer,
my next life.

What I Didn't Know

I didn't know my father's sisters raised their children
to believe our grandfather was dead.

How had this never come up until a college-age conversation
with my cousin after he really was dead? Angry
at the deception, she lamented the loss.

I didn't know he had left his wife and children,
that my aunts had armed a wall against him,
that when their mother died, and their father showed up
at her funeral after many absent years,
my aunts made my father turn him away—
the biggest regret my father said he ever had—

Since my mother could not live with a man who had regrets,
she found his vanished father,
years before the internet would have made it easy,
and raised her children to know him
and his new wife—
my beloved grandmother,
his floozy.

III

Unspoken

I

Your rolled stockings, Lysol smell, chicken
soup. You with your big black shoe looking
for one of us grandkids to smack. You never
stopped talking, talking about our messy
apartment downstairs from you: seven people
in three small rooms. You tried to hold us
against each other as we grew.

II

I lean close to your better ear, say my words
louder this time, maybe you'll hear.
My husband, uncomfortable
on your plastic-covered couch, asks,
Why wear yourself out?

III

Your feet propped on the green hassock
by the window of the Bronx apartment
your children moved you to. Arthritis
and bunions wrap your toes over each other
the way we used to cross our fingers
when we wanted something badly or lied.

The teeth I found on your dresser doily
next to the empty pill bottles when I
was seven. Your maybe-almost-suicide.
Mom says yes, Aunt Fran still says no.

IV

Peter's wedding is November 4th,
I will wear my blue dress. And then I will die,
and you will not have to visit me anymore.

You state this matter-of-factly, satisfied,
maybe at how awkward it makes me feel.

V

Aunt Cary and Aunt Venera visited as a pair
my entire life. Cary, my mother's cousin,
and Venera, her "roommate," my mother always
said and believed. But you say you knew
the truth about them all along,
it's just the way it was.

VI

I cut your hair. The silver sheen, strands
so thick and strong, I can't go wrong.

Grandpa wouldn't talk to me for a week
after I bobbed it.

You say it proudly. And suddenly become,
not my Grandma, but a young flapper
defying her husband.

In the steamer trunk you direct me to, I find,
laid in a box, a long brown braid, bristled
and preserved.

You stroke the rope of hair I bring you.

VII

Little John died when he was three, you say,
so at forty you birthed my Uncle John. I wonder
what my uncle thought of being named for his dead
brother, but you are already on to another story
of the girl, you, outside the bakery, how the baker
said he would marry you, and your mother said,
Yes, you will always have bread.

VIII

The photo on your dresser captures your
so-very-oldness next to your young son.
The only Uncle John I knew, twelve
when Susan was born, fourteen when I fell
through his fingers, fractured my small skull.
You brought me a brown teddy bear.
Its hard-plastic face, pouting, a teardrop
frozen on its cheek.

IX

I always find you in the green armchair
by the window gazing at the brownstone
across the street. The same one in which,
I discover, you raised your children, married off
your daughters, lost one John and birthed another.

What do you see all day, staring.

X

I am surprised to learn that you, my Italian
grandmother, were born in Florida. That
the family returned to Sicily because your father
had a tumor in his nose. That the doctor
said he'd get better there. That he died
on your fifth birthday. That your mother
took the family back to Tampa alone.
That you were one of five, like me.

When I say your mother must have been
brave, you reply, *Yes, that is why we all named
a daughter after her.*

And suddenly I know her name, and why I had
five aunts named Frances.

XI

Your mother rolled cigars in Ybor City. Your
mouth mixed Spanish, Italian, English. You show
me a small snapshot, 1923 penned above two teenage
girls, one White, one Black.

Me, you say, pointing, *and my best friend.*

XII

The hospital room smells sour. The tracheotomy
hole in your throat reminds me of cookies, a perfect
circle cut in dough, cookies we might have baked
together had we been different.

Sunken, silenced mouth. Sans eyeglasses,
hearing aids, teeth, you lie unseeing and soundless.

XIII

For ninety-two years you followed
someone else's vision of your life.
You crossed an ocean, married for bread.
But I have met the woman who bobbed her hair.

When you look at me, I know you want to see
the son you lost, your husband gone twenty-two years,
your brothers and sisters, your mother.

You are trapped in your body
by your children's need for your survival.
The tube stuck in your throat's tired folds.
I hold your hand.

XIV

Emptying your apartment, I find fifty
flat bed sheets, once white, still ribbon-wrapped,
stacked in the linen closet.

Shall I cover the Bronx in real sheets of metaphorical
snow? Bind the ozone layer? Tie them end to end
and help you climb down from heaven? Cut eyeholes,
slip the sheet over my head, become a ghost, and visit?

For my grandmother, Maria Cammarata DiPalermo,
  March 25, 1903-December 15, 1995

IV

We Were Young Together
Ode to Wayne 1959-2011

The boy in the white house, two
houses down, showed me
his blistered back, his father's strap.
He'd help me up the hill, then push me
down. Throw rocks at my head. Ring
doorbells and run.

Days became years became nights
my windows pebbled till I climbed out.
Making crank calls, hanging up, snorting
laughter and beer, hanging out for hours
on the rusted lawn chairs in his backyard.

A Marlboro always between his lips
that never touched mine. I'd watch
the tip burn, the way he'd squint
when he drew the smoke in.

We'd pass warm vodka, kill time,
use his long string of girlfriends
to drive us around.

I must have seen him in something other
than his brown leather jacket, tee shirt
and jeans, but that is all I remember. I can still
smell the jacket and cigarettes, see his yellow-
tinged fingers.

I cried on his shoulder over every boyfriend,
he could be so gentle. I have a photo of him
taken in my bedroom, holding my stuffed bear
when we were too old for such things.

His eyes were blue, his hands scraped
from tending his garden. He always lit up
his father's house for Christmas, the festive
package wrapping the hell he lived within.
He never came to school. We talked
but never talked.

When I was away at college, he'd call, late
in my dorm, slurring words. But home, he was
always there in the white house. Now it was bars
and clubs instead of lawn chairs. But it was
the same, even when he got his girlfriend pregnant,
even when they moved to Florida, even when I pointed
down the block, saying to a visiting boyfriend,
that white house is where my friend Wayne lived...
and stopped because it was yellow
and there were little kids playing out front.

He followed me long before Facebook,
through my two marriages, random late-night calls
until the one from his wife:
Wayne is dead. We're bringing him home...

Wayne in the casket, looking like he just passed out.

Sisters

You know she was as unlike you as the sea and sun.
You know from stories that when your mother
carried you home, cradled your skull in its pink bonnet,
she turned from you and kept turning.

Maybe it began there.

Or perhaps there is no true beginning, only a continuation,
this time louder, reverberating longer.

She asks amends in one email, screams accusations in the next.
She gets married and doesn't tell you,
then sends photos of what you missed.

You know you shared the same house, parents, brothers,
but never thoughts or secrets.
You know you never knew her
and even one summer pretended

she was not your sister, like you wish you could now
when someone asks how many siblings you have
and you don't know how to answer.

You know it is not—yet somehow is—your fault,
something never whole
cannot be broken.

You know everyone agrees she is not to be trusted,
there is the litany of terrible things she has done,

which you know she sees as justified.

You know everything about her and nothing
of who she is, how she is,
why she is as she is, and can never be
the sister you wish you had.

A Letter to My High School Sweetheart

I can't imagine what you are like now,
can see only a version of you that may be
as false as the one you had of me.

I find photographs: me lifted in your arms
as if you were catching me, or were you
tossing me away? Me: holding your
brother's soccer ball like I cared, your
shirt open, cigarette unlit between lips,
brown eyes, those long and curling lashes.
Me again, in that horrible pink gown my mother
got on sale for prom, you in your matching
pink ruffled shirt and maroon tux. I forgot
they made lapels that big.

And here's our prom photo, my little brother
sitting between us, who accompanied me
for reasons too complicated to explain, yet,
I realize now,
you never questioned,
I realize now,
that was love.

Hearing It for the First Time

My brothers laugh when they tell it:
Our father pounding on their locked door,

locomotive, Peter squared against it,
pushing back, Adam kneeling by the bottom bunk,

his face, where he'd picked it, bright pellet holes.
Nobody remembers what they'd done, just

the burst as the hinges popped
and our father became for a moment

Aladdin, riding the door to the floor
in a flash of dust.

Estranged

You work so hard little brother—
your head protruding through memories of hair

the day we caught you without your cap,
your eyes brown still

reflecting not on who we once were
but moving forward to where you will be

after the next great plan is realized.
You who once tied me

to the doorpost and hurled
steak knives at my unflinching body

I trusted you that much.
"Do you and Paul talk?" a friend

once asked. Not of things that bind us,
that leave us wondering about this life that grew

around us. Our talk turns to nods
and moving things we catch for a moment

before they are gone.

Still Life

There is the laughing bronze Buddha,
hand over mouth, hand on belly.
Here is the photo of my brother's wife,
pregnant with twins, smiling,
hand holding up shirt, hand on belly.

After the boys were born, she showed
me her belly, deflated flesh, grabbed
a chunk of it in her hands, hands
now holding Ryan, holding Lucas,
mouth smiling, singing, their hands

not quite yet grasping her hands,
her long hair. She is a temple of calm
as they scream—tiny legs curling
into tiny chests, faces red. She strokes
their bellies.

Behind my Buddha, the marble boy
reading. Both Buddha and the boy
small enough to slip into a handbag.
The boy bought in a small shop in Pisa,
found in a bin of leaning towers.

The Buddha cast in a small shop
in Greenwich Village. Between them
a candle, purple, brought home
from our Louisiana wedding. The boy
and the Buddha and the candle sit

near the double-volume OED case, with
its slim blue drawer and magnifying glass,
and a paper copy of me in my wedding dress,
beautiful. The photo creased, collapsing.
A red and white trade-show ball, *Fits in your hand,*

squeeze when stressed, sits in front of the photo.
The OED and the boy and the Buddha
and the candle and the stress ball are wedged
between two bookshelves, both overfull
like Buddha's belly and my sister-in-law's.

This is our life here in these objects—what is there
but music, reading, travel, learning? There is
the candle we burn, my favorite color, there is
the happiest day, there is the stress. But here
is the photo that can never be me: smiling, hand over belly.

Plastic Pearls

Red high heels, plastic pearls,
a weekend's worth of Beauty

and the Beast, Lion King, Snow
White, and my sister's child.

Rocking, rocking her body
buckled in the back seat of my car,

her wail low now
almost a hum with the tires.

She doesn't care
about my grand experiment

in motherhood, knows only
her mother vanished.

Reception After Communion

After my nephew's First Holy Communion,
my three brothers' wives table together,

heads bowed, whispering, sisters to each other
with our last name. My sister and I join,

strangers among them, passing sugar.

Advice

The tone of my nephew's text was desperate.
He needed my advice—So why not give freely
my hard-gained wisdom? My amazing insight?
What only I could bestow on his crippling agony,
crushed ego?

His girlfriend had dumped him--
after seven *fantastic* dates—the shock of it.
He had dined and wined her, sent flowers, thought her
the most beautiful, gave her more than he ever had given
his ex-wife, mother of his children, who wished, wailed
and waited for ten years for a bouquet or a thank you.

But no, he is a changed man, would show himself new
to the next woman, till each in turn left him. He forwards
me their text exchange, the reply he wants to send:
why? why? why?

So, as with his mother, my sister, I drop everything
to read through their words and what he cannot yet see,
why not to send it, how I know this. The next day
he texts that five others he asked said the same thing,
but he sent it anyway.

V

Our Mother Always Told Us She Had Lots of Boyfriends

Did we ever believe her?
All we saw was our mother who'd grown
short, squat and grey with the five of us.

Did she exist before that? An impossible girl
buying milk in glass bottles for her father,
saving nickels for a red dress with a tulle skirt,
dreaming on the number 5 subway of Sicilian olive groves?

When I'd ask why she chose our father, she'd say
she wanted children. She was already 29. Her cousins
and friends had married. She didn't want to be
an old maid. She didn't want to marry.
He was the best choice.
Sometimes she'd say this in front of our father,
who always said he married her because
she looked like Ava Gardner.

One day I found her in photographs,
in the cardboard suitcase in the attic.
Lipsticked laughing, on a beach brushing brown hair,
leaning on a doorway, eyes half moons,
sitting on the shoulders, of a man
not my father.

My Parents, Aging Together

Their first date was to a sci-fi movie he loved
and she hated. That should have been a warning.
He says she looked like Ava Gardner, and I wonder
what he thinks now that she looks like a pear
that's sat in the refrigerator too long.

She says nothing about how he looked,
though pictures show he was handsome,
just that he was a nice Irish boy who
didn't tell her what to do all the time.

He loves movies, cards and board games.
His idea of heaven is the bus to Atlantic City
where he can ride for free, watch the little TV
and eat Milky Ways despite his diabetes.

She loves reading and traveling.
Her idea of heaven is being the oldest person
in the Ph.D. program at Columbia University
and telling them to stick it up their ass
if they don't like it.

Powdered sugar is sprinkled like dandruff
over his shirtfront when I visit. He never
looks at himself, so he doesn't notice
this or the white V-necked undershirt
that doesn't line up with the askew collar
on his blue shirt. If she were home,
she'd tell him and he'd fix it, but she's off

doing something he doesn't even try
to keep up with. He's been remaking
Grandma's old couch, he explains happily.
He's pulled out all the springs and stuffing
and created a surprisingly Danish-like
wooden couch. "Mom will make cushions,"
he says, in an equally weird version
of domesticity acquired after forty-five years.

This weekend they escape to my house
where they rub together in the small rooms
till all our hair stands on end. He reads the map,
trying to locate the best way to get to the park.
She wants to see Hamlet, even though we all know
his snores will disrupt the outdoor production.
I suggest they do something they both will enjoy.
He holds the small plastic magnifying glass
attached to his key ring against the thin blue lines
and mumbles that he can't find Route 22, and I repeat,
"It's there, I've driven it." Resist the urge to grab
the map from his hands. Even across the room, I can
find the route. She says he doesn't listen, but he
can't hear and refuses to believe it. When I complain
to her about the donuts and his hearing, she says it's his life.

They go to Hamlet where he falls asleep and she gets mad.

She tries not to show that she's in love with my husband.
When I echoed her frustrations, during the eight years
of my first marriage, she'd sigh, say marriage is no picnic,
women are fed fairytales, there is no Prince Charming.

So, when I brought home my new husband, she seemed
dazed and betrayed that I had found someone with whom
life could be a picnic, that I had enacted the fairytale.

She is, of course, happy for my happiness, but I think
if she had to do it all again, she would have chosen
the second man I married. And he may have
chosen her if he had been alive then. After all, aren't I
the best parts of her? It was dumb luck that he and I
stumbled into each other's arms. Or else I would be
saying this is how marriage is, you know,
whoever said it was a picnic?

The Photo

Taken of my parents and me on the gangplank
of a restored Paddlewheel Riverboat. One of those photos
venders take without asking, then charge you to keep.

My father has this photo, framed on his dresser.
My mother's hair, golden where the sun has caught it,
her mouth wide, smiling. My father next to her, holding
her jacket in front of him. And the jagged cut between them,
where he'd scissored me out of the picture
and pasted the two of them together.

My Father Comes To My Poetry Reading

"What did you think?"

"Your poems are like stories."

"Yes," I say.

"But real poetry rhymes," he says.
"I like poems that rhyme."

VI

Still Life with Chairs

The chair only my father sat in.
Brown? Beige? Woven. Rough and worn
where his arms rested after another long day
standing and slicing, stacking salami, pastrami.
My father should have had a La-Z-Boy recliner
lifting his feet and bearing him like a sultan.

My mother hauled his chair home from a Bronxville Street
on garbage day. But I cannot see the chair, only my father:
head thrown back, voluminous snores that roared through
  our house
until we changed the TV channel, then like Moby Dick
surfacing, he'd sputter and snort, *"I was watching that!"*

The chair only my mother sat in.
Wood. Armless so she could reach the kitchen table
that served as her desk, books and papers piled so high
we'd use them as fort walls for toy soldiers.
The chair, empty mostly. She never sat until we went to bed,
sleeping to the typewriter's rat tat tat.

This was the chair that held her dreams,
one spindle split after my brother threw it at his twin.
Her chair broken and the five of us trying to break her—
to make her like everyone else's mother.

We demanded, whined, hated her so hard
because she wouldn't bake cookies or make *SpaghettiOs*
or wear an apron, dragged us to museums, libraries,

71

tried to tell us an empty refrigerator box was better
than a Barbie. And only when it became puppet theater,
house or car did we believe her.

She rose mightily from that chair.

One Moment

My father drops my mother at the subway,
heading to the job she refused to retire
from, and kisses her goodbye. She climbs
the stairs thinking of the day's deadlines,
the weather she did not want to walk through.
The doors swallow her.

In the hospital room after the frantic
family phone calls, she sleeps,
a pillow wedged between hip and bar,
hands pricked with needles.

I watch the steady pulse of breath,
of machines pumping. Half-eaten turkey
and sweet potatoes mashed on the tray.

A woman comes in to mop and whispers,
Today is her birthday. I shake my head.
Yes, she insists. *She told me she is 70 today.*

A dozen years and two months younger
than fact.

My Italian Catholic Human Rights Commissioner Mother

Her room empty, I search
the nursing home halls panicked,
eye the elderly, caved-in people
parked around the nurses' station,
demand to know where she is.

A nurse points to a nearby wheelchair:
the woman collapsed inside.
My mother?

I touch her paper skin, hold her hand,
caress the jade Claddagh ring
I brought her from Ireland.
Her green eyes light then die.
I wheel her back to her room.

My mother, my anarchist.

I am nobody, she says.

I upend my backpack.
Her books and papers tumble
between the bars
of her narrow bed.

I hand her a copy of an article she wrote.
She reads it twice and returns to me
her old self,
before the fall.

She grows angry at her legs,
raises her fists, her mouth a hard knot.

I will remind her who she is
every time she forgets.

An Impossible Secret

My mother's decades-younger brother
is suddenly dead. The family clamps down
around her—mum's the word. They ignore
my argument, her right to know, insist
it would just depress her.

But we no longer know what she thinks.
She has lost the ability or willingness
to speak. It feels like she is mad at us.
Like the silent treatment she punished
us with as children. It feels
exactly like that.

But her right to know gnaws at me.
Will she wonder why he no longer visits?
Convinced, as she said once after we fired
yet another unreliable aide,
that she is why everyone leaves?

At her brother's funeral I guide my father
to the grave's gaping hole, try to fill
her gaping absence.

Weeks later she sits wheelchaired close
as I recount her medical and family history
to her new neurologist. As the words leave
my lips, I realize that I have stated her
brother's heart attack and death. I look at her
and she gazes at me, just gazes.

My Mother's Diary, Found Sunday

I am the book that holds her words,
her words that held her mind
steady and rapt in 1999 when her son's sons
curled and cried and she was so very tired,
holding one then the other through the night
while their mother tried to sleep,
their birth still heavy on her shattered breath.

She told me things she never told you.

I am so full of her and who she was and will
never be again. Pages fall out of me and you
can't stuff them back. I knew her better than you—
the peculiar way she underlined passages, left out
words. I never questioned only took what
she poured into me out of her. Blue smears
across my broadside, words across lines. Nothing
in her mind yet crossed out, deleted, destroyed.

I Am

not the body that's left
staring at I don't know what
holding up holding back
holding on

my body's hired keeper
cleans my shit chooses
my clothes the white
sensible shoes I always hated
laced tight

my husband still
makes meatloaf with extra
onions plays cards
fanned in my hand
I always hated cards

my firstborn gloats she is now
my favorite hides me
from all others I ever
loved her sister just tries tries
cries

and my sons my sons my wardens
prop my diminished body into
existence

none of you can see me—
you see me only as I am not

but I am a person not a thing

the heart you called home.

Hands Unfolded in Prayer, Beseeching

It is a blessing, really, the end
after years of failing, the way
we stood around her, distant shadows
of someone she knew or might have known,
her children's erased faces. It is a blessing
against the glare of a faded light. But
this body before me was home.
Still

we bless the body, pack away
her lilted laughter climbing
the stairs, remember the time when....
Wishing

just once
to see her again
as she was.
Rising

before us to get her work done,
comb our hair,
hug us long and hard,
her voice saying,
Good morning.

My Mother's Jewelry

Two hands clasped a jade-crowned heart,
green, like her eyes. I leaned over the jewelry
counter at Clery's in Dublin and pointed
to the gold Claddagh ring I wanted
for my mother.

I was nineteen and she had told me to go
even though I was scared. She scraped
money from I don't know where
and signed me up to discover the heritage
even my father didn't know, although his
father and every father before had come
from some Irish county.

Three months later I brought her back
the ring and was a woman she said
she almost did not recognize
as I emerged through the gate.

She wore that ring every day. And
the silver floating heart necklace that hung
on a looped chain, from my father on their 50th.
She would joke it was the only jewelry
he ever gave her, which wasn't true.
I remember the Tweety Bird earrings.

And who gave her the silver charm bracelet?
Each charm a milestone: tiny typewriter, twin
baby shoes. The house, smaller than on my

Monopoly set. I don't remember what charm
meant me, but surely there was one.

And she never took off her grandmother's
hoop earrings from Sicily. These things
were so much a part of her we never noticed
they were parted from her, never missed them
until we were missing her. Were they pocketed
at the home or hospital? Pawned for a living
wage by any of her caretakers?

Just a memory now, like her, forever gone.

Until my brother opened a plastic pouch
and dropped into my palm her wedding band
and diamond engagement ring she always told me
she'd paid for because my father couldn't,
even then betting his meager wages
on a sure win and the promise
she never broke to stand by him.

She outgrew them in the Seventies,
tucked them away for safe keeping.

Forever something to hold now, something to have.

For my mother, Marianne DiPalermo McCauley,
  August 26, 1927-November 2, 2012

A Year After My Mother's Death

Hours stuffed into a clock, disappear.
It is my second month teaching dance at sea.
The students are all my mother and father.

World War II vets bend over walkers, hope
for a last glimpse of bare-breasted brown
women from their days in the South Pacific.

One tells me sixteen passengers died
on his last world cruise. Long voyages,
a new way of assisted living, they drop
port by port, seven so far. Yesterday
my husband mentioned he hasn't seen
our neighbor's scooter plugged
into the hallway lately.

I walk the deck at night, watch the sea
churn, a black hole easy to slip into.

A man my age tells me he has
already been dead. I ask if he saw
the mythical light. He shakes his head
but says the scars on his chest
form an upside-down smiley face,
do I want to see it?

There are five dance hosts aboard
who travel for free but must dance
with single ladies six hours a day.

One confides his Alzheimer's.
Is he kidding? He is fifty-seven.
Early onset, he tells me.

I begin to feel my strong limbs
and breath, foreign. I wake early, alone
among Filipinos who vacuum and polish,
serve us more food than they could imagine
at home. When we walk in their country,
hammocks and clothes are strung
along trafficked streets. Naked children try
to sell us golf balls landed over the country
club fence. A girl umbrella-shades a golfer
for a few pesos. In another day the Philippines
will be devastated by typhoon. I will imagine
them all washed onto the green. But today
I photograph Fort Manila's famous gates,
try to shoot around underwear hung on a line,
people living in the shadows.

Typhoon Haiyan reroutes us to Nagasaki,
where uniformed schoolgirls smile
in front of the atomic bomb monument.

And in a school room in Papua, New Guinea,
descendants of cannibals scramble all over me
to see their image on my phone.

I teach a dance step. They wiggle and laugh.
Their bare chests and faces painted,
feathers in their hair, eyes surprisingly green.

Emptying My Parents' House

In the photo taken long ago
and a moment ago, my mother and I

stand, still together, smiling,
at the top of the stairs in front of our house,

the house now sold by my brothers
while I was away, giving me one day to say

goodbye to the rooms now empty of us.
We all lived so large in that house.

Curtains red like the bleeding heart
my father always accused me of being

and orange like my mother's pantsuit circa 1970.
Memories crisscross each other as I pack—

blur time, signs lost and followed...
The giving up, the never giving up.

all of it now: stacked, stored, divided.
In my old room the alarm clock ticks.

My toes are cold. The scarves
my mother had draped by the window flutter

from the heating duct below.
I watch them lift and surrender.

VII

On Taking Our 84-Year-Old Dad To Six Flags

There was a time he stood
    us on his shoes
so we'd be tall enough
    for the Dragon Coaster
our mom screaming
    all the way down laughing
all the way up that hiccup laugh
    she had my brothers laughing
all of us screaming and laughing
    going after each other
smashing bumper cars
    running through
the House of Mirrors

Now he plows his rented scooter
    through the crowd
leaves it
    in the middle of the path
at the Bumper Cars where he
    cannot remember how to
make his car go he circles backwards
    my brother bumps him forward
the other back again until he frees
    himself finds himself becomes
himself finally again
    we follow him to the Log Flume
my brothers holding each elbow as he steps in
    sits as I snuggle against him

screaming laughing then water soaked
     we head toward the "Elvis" show
music so loud we plug our ears but
     he sits upfront mesmerized
afterward marvels how well
     he heard without his hearing aid
Almost too loud! he tells me over
     and over again as he hops back
on his scooter takes off
     Wait! we yell but he can't hear
can't stop can only leave us behind.

Forgetting

It's not that I can't remember
her face, a kaleidoscope
of pictures pressed into an album
in my mind—bunched and indiscriminate—
here, a proud mother,
there a young bride.
I can even date them—
the square black-and-whites,
the faded polaroids,
and the oh-so-many Kodak moments
missing heads, hands or feet.

My mother at the stove,
phone cord wrapped
around her body, that ridiculous
orange and green kitchen
prompting me to think taste
must have gone missing
for an entire decade.

It's not like I don't recall, when I hear
a high-pitched screech while walking
through a playground, the shriek
of her laughter
on the Dragon Coaster
when we were kids
and cajoled her to join us.

It's not that I can no longer feel

the cool comfort of her arms,
moist lips on my forehead,
eruption of fear and giggles
when she chased Paul
with the wooden spoon.

But how to forget the imprint
of her diminishing?
Losing her day by day until
she was altogether gone.

Hello

When you arrive at the communion party
under a big tent in your nephew's yard,
you say a general hello to everyone
at the round rented table where your sister
and her latest husband sit, a wedding
you were not invited to. You say hello
to her daughter, your niece, who has driven
up from North Carolina. Say hello to her friend,
whom she lives with but who is not her boyfriend,
although he has driven them here and she
is supporting him through school. Hello
to your sister, whom you only started
speaking to again before her mastectomy.
Her husband does not look at you,
so you don't say hello to him. Later,
your sister pulls you aside and says her husband
wants to leave and it's all your fault because
you didn't say hello. He thinks you hate him.
You do. But that is beside the point.

At first you explain that you said hello to everyone
who said hello to you, that hellos are, after all,
reciprocal. But then you give up being right,
and follow her to her husband and say, *Hello, Hello.*

Suddenly, he cannot do enough for you.
He brings you soda and chips. Offers you
ice. The next day your aunt, who didn't go
to the party, calls to say your sister called her
to report how you didn't even say hello.

Leaning Over Infinity

I feel foolish—
    wasted time, breath, bother
the years my sister and I
didn't speak to understand
    but to better, judge, doubt—
how she didn't invite me
    to her wedding because she knew
    I would say not to marry him
how I stopped listening
    because there was nothing
    about her way of being
    I could understand
how she would agree
    with my sage advice
    then do whatever she wanted
how I cringed at her choices
how I just let voicemail pick up
how reaching back
    into our childhood
    all we shared
    was a deep divide
how I envied other sisters—
    the fantasy of closeness
    and connection
how she was never
    my sister
    but a weight I carried
how she died
    alone in her son's living

room and he went to work
without noticing.

For my sister, March 9, 1959-June 12, 2018

Jumbled

8mm films watched so often I wonder
if I'm recalling the movie or the moments.

My sister's high school graduation,
the closeup of her, pleased and proud,
eyes casting away from the camera,
her dress white and lacy, a flower in her hair.

And the footage known in family lore as
the "Shootout at the O.K. Corral." My three
little brothers in cowboy hats, in the dirt yard
of the rented Lake George trailer, drawing
cap guns, outdoing each other clutching
wounds, dropping in dramatic death throes.

Unlabeled 8mm reels jumbled in a box
became a single DVD, a copy for each of us,
a gift from our father after our mother died.
Holidays and special occasions preserved,
as if those were the only days that mattered.

But no one filmed us waiting endlessly for Mom
to get out of work, the boys climbing
City Hall's eight-foot black iron fence,
each rail a spear, me calling, "Time to go!"
Peter jumping down, impaling his right palm
until it ripped through. Or my father dropping
me and my best friend, Wendy, at the library
for "our important assignment," although I was

grounded. How he lay in wait, turned the headlights
on us as we rounded the block on our way to
our boyfriends' thinking we were so smart.

Yet, we have film of every week-long vacation
to housekeeping cottages my mother always found,
always requesting the scenic route, my father obliging.

No camera caught us station-wagon stuffed,
four of us backseat belted by twos, one buckled
upfront with Mom, the dog panting in our faces.

Or Adam rocking, rocking his body against
the seatback, vibrations all over, me carsick,
whining to my mother, Peter punching Adam
to stop, Paul punching Peter, Peter punching
him back, Susan turning up her transistor radio,
my mother trying to get us to play "I See,"
my father threatening to stop the car and leave us there.

Or the Pennsylvania drive-in theatre my father
wouldn't take us to, saying we could see
the screen from the front porch of our cottage
and he'd grown up with silent movies:
here was our chance to see one.

There is no footage of that long drive to Maine.
My mother had no idea how winding the roads,
the air thick and fogging, the five of us
begging to stop at a motel, my father determined,
my mother hanging out the window with a flashlight

to help him see, till finally we arrived, parked
in the black, the next morning found the car
almost in the lake.

Or my favorite, *The Ranch*, somewhere
in the Catskills. Booked so off-season, we were
the only guests there. Cute ranch-hands, bored,
spent hours entertaining my thirteen-year-old
sister and me. I decided they were in love with us.
One night they planted a white glove on a stick
rising from the ground, shined a flashlight on it,
then tapped, tapped, tapped on our window.
I can still hear that tap.

Am I still the me sprawled on the floor
in the living room with my brothers
and sister waiting for our father to unfurl the great
screen, thread film onto sprockets, our mother
making popcorn, burnt and burdened by hard kernels.

We'd point each other out on screen as if a revelation:
Look at Peter! Look at Adam! Look at Susan!
Look at Paul! But thinking, *Look at me!*

On our new DVD, my sister's first wedding is followed
by her baptism followed by her high school graduation—
our linear lives fractured. We see my sister's druggie
boyfriend, Louie, lurking in New Hampshire, my last
family vacation. No one filmed the fights to get her
to come with us.

Or the bicycle the twins took without telling anyone.
How Peter skidded to a stop and Adam, perched behind him,
flew over his head, over the handlebars, sliding face first
against gravel. It was painful to look at him. But we see
no hospital scene, just us scampering about Story Land Park,
Adam hooded in a sweatshirt, his face swollen beyond
   recognition,
unable to smile.

After my sister's funeral, our mother already gone
six years, we gathered in Peter's living room.
He brought out the DVD. It was hours long.
My father grew restless. My sisters-in-law
drifted back into the kitchen, the children
to their computer games.

But my brothers and I sat, mesmerized
by ourselves.

Someone I Love Is Dying

and the children we were bow their heads
to the past, each holding dear
a particular image of our father
that the others do not share. Because
I am older, I've known him longer
and different. Even before his belly
and the brief year of the generous moustache
that made him look like a Greek fisherman
instead of the pale Irishman he was
who pickled at the beach, who had
so many arms and legs for all five of us
to hang onto as the ocean beat us
back to sand. There was the year
of teaching me to drive, my fingers
gripping the giant steering wheel,
his ancient Cadillac a boat under us
as he instructed me to back slowly
into an impossible sleeve. My brothers
do not know this particular man
in that particular moment, just as
I do not know their own moments
with our father. When I was very young,
before my brothers were born, our father
was still our father, shared with my sister,
but since she's gone, it's just me
and the boys. I've been the only girl
for three years now, and although
my brothers are younger, they live
in a kind of masculine authority

over me and our father. Our father
whose body is clearly giving up hope.
As much as we have seen of our father,
none of us have ever seen him like this.
And the feeling of not knowing how
to save him has each of us by the throat.

For my father, Thomas McCauley,
*   December 20, 1930-August 5, 2021*

Home Again

A grey squirrel sits where the tree house was.
Broken slats nailed to the bark hang loose as if now
even the tree allowed no girls to ascend.

Going back requires hope and defies
longing, is never a return to what was
but to what is now not.

Memory bends and stretches, shapes
a new creation: the loves lovelier,
the hurts harsher.

The lattice under the porch
where *that damn woodchuck* lived
with her yearly crop of babies is gone,

the hours inside the house are gone,
but the door is still there, blown open,
and the green shutters still cling,

though most of the windows are broken.
Stories told and retold over time,
each slightly different, each absolutely true.

The grass my father never mowed. How
the boyfriend who became my husband who became
my ex-husband who became the father of a child
he never wanted with me—fertilized
the front yard and planted ivy so my father

would not have to mow. Who knew

the ivy's long locks would choke the wall,
destroy the mortar? How each turn of my life
became a new road without my ever seeing
its one-way sign.